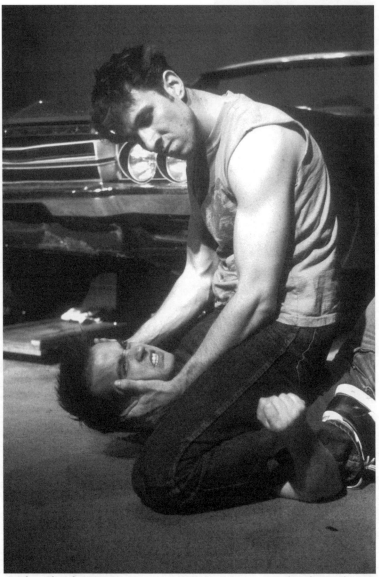

Pablo T. Scheiber and Brian Sacca in a scene
from the New York production of *Blood Orange*.

BLOOD ORANGE

BY DAVID WIENER

★

DRAMATISTS
PLAY SERVICE
INC.

for my mom

BLOOD ORANGE premiered in New York City at The Cherry Lane Theater on March 11, 2001. It was directed by Anders Cato. The cast was as follows:

CLINTON	Pablo T. Schreiber
RAY-RAY	Brian Sacca
THE GIRL	Julienne Hanzelka Kim
ERNIE-BOBO	Johnathan Hova
ANGELA	Wendy vanden Heuvel
JILL	Susan Peligrino
LINDA	Julia Gibson

BLOOD ORANGE was subsequently presented by the Development Wing (Robert Kravitz, Evangeline Morphos, Noel Ashman and Karen Davidov) at The Blue Heron in New York City on May 20, 2001. It was directed by Anders Cato; the set design was by John McDermott; the costume design was by Richard Pierce; the lighting design was by Justin Burleson; the sound design was by Roger Raines; the production stage manager was Paul A. Kochman; and the assistant stage manager was Bob Knapp; the technical director was Adrian Gallard; the fight coordinator was Paul Molnar; the line producer was Sherri Kotimsky; the general manager was Steven Chaikelson; the company manager was Karina Miller; and the associate producers were Jason Kahan, Claire Kelly, Richard Rothenberg and Adam Ernster. The cast was as follows:

CLINTON	Pablo T. Schreiber
RAY-RAY	Brian Sacca
THE GIRL	Julienne Hanzelka Kim
ERNIE-BOBO	Johnathan Hova
ANGELA	Wendy vanden Heuvel
JILL	Susan Peligrino
LINDA	Ilene Kristen

CHARACTERS

RAY-RAY / RAY — 17, dark curly hair

CLINTON — 19, muscled

THE GIRL — 14, pretty, with a bad dye-job

JILL — mid-40s, Clinton's mom

ANGELA — mid-40s, Ray-Ray's mom

LINDA — mid-30s, The Girl's mom

ERNIE-BOBO — 17, with a mild mental disability

PLACE

Orange County.

TIME

1983.

Note on the Set: The only set piece is the car. For the sake of speedy transitions, the play benefits from a non-naturalistic staging and a minimum of set and prop concerns.

BLOOD ORANGE

ACT ONE

Lights up. Ray stands down stage.

RAY. He caught me on the lawn
beneath the womanly old arms of the pine
He was bigger and older than I
This was in the summer of infinite heat
after Proposition 13
after Richard Ramirez
when everyone was divorced *(Lights up on a car. Late at night. Clinton is at the wheel. Ernie-Bobo sits shotgun with a map.)*
ERNIE-BOBO. Pa-Pa had a metal mouth. All metal. 'Cause his teeth was metal. 'Cause he chewed the 'baco and it turned his teeth metal. And he was old. He was old. He was older than tel-vision and he watched the tel-vision. And did his squirt. Brown squirt in the squirt bowl. And watch the tel-vision. And let me sit on him. And, and one time — and one time he did his squirt. Like this. He did his squirt and his metal. He did his squirt and dink. Like that. The shiny tooth dink in the shiny bowl. And he laughed. He laughed. His face got crinkle and he put his finger in the bowl. He laughed 'cause metal teeth is funny sometimes. And he gave it to me. And he laughed and put it on a string. And it's mine. It's mine for keeps. And when. And one time. And when he was in the box. He went in the box 'cause he was old. And the Moms and Ron. Ron is my second dad. I have four dads. And Mike. I don't see Mike no more. And we saw Pa-Pa in the box. And Pa-Pa was in the box. And Mom said the box was a far far. A far far far far far far far better place than here. And Pa-Pa. And I walked up to Pa-Pa. And he was a dead man. And I went. I got in trouble. And one time. I tried to put the metal tooth in his dead mouth. And I got in trou-

7

ble 'cause you know better than to touch a dead man. Pa-Pa went into the ground. Which is in the Earth. Which is green.

CLINTON. Shut up.

ERNIE-BOBO. Sorry Clinton.

CLINTON. Just be quiet. *(Pause.)*

ERNIE-BOBO. *(Sing-song.)* Bo, bo, bo, bo, bo, bo, bo, bo —

CLINTON. Fuck. You're gonna ruin it. You're ruining it.

ERNIE-BOBO. Sorry Clinton.

CLINTON. Turn the radio on. *(Ernie-Bobo does.)* Damn. We got another hour 'till we hit the border. Check for fuzz. *(Ernie-Bobo leans out the window and looks back.)* All clear?

ERNIE-BOBO. All clear.

CLINTON. I'm gonna let her out a little.

ERNIE-BOBO. Okay. *(Pause.)* Are we going fast?

CLINTON. Of course we're going fast. We're fucking flying. Look out the window.

ERNIE-BOBO. Okay.

CLINTON. You see all those trees?

ERNIE-BOBO. No.

CLINTON. Look again.

ERNIE-BOBO. I see.

CLINTON. And?

ERNIE-BOBO. They're all blurry.

CLINTON. That's right.

ERNIE-BOBO. Fast.

CLINTON. Damn fast. We're doing a hundred miles an hour. We'll be in Baja by breakfast.

ERNIE-BOBO. Faster.

CLINTON. You want me to go faster?

ERNIE-BOBO. Faster.

CLINTON. Okay. There. One oh five.

ERNIE-BOBO. Faster.

CLINTON. Faster?

ERNIE-BOBO. Go faster.

CLINTON. You sure?

ERNIE-BOBO. Yeah.

CLINTON. I'm telling you, we hit a slick spot and we're dead.

ERNIE-BOBO. Faster.

CLINTON. I don't know man. Could be risky. *(Ernie-Bobo checks for the fuzz.)*

ERNIE-BOBO. All clear.

CLINTON. All right. Hold on to your ass.

ERNIE-BOBO. Faster.

CLINTON. Are you crazy? We're doing fifty over the limit.

ERNIE-BOBO. Faster.

CLINTON. You're a speed freak, you know that?

ERNIE-BOBO. Speed freak.

CLINTON. Fuck it. Let's see what she can do. One oh seven.

ERNIE-BOBO. Ahhhhhhh!

CLINTON. One ten!

ERNIE-BOBO. Ahhhhhhh!

CLINTON. One twelve!

ERNIE-BOBO. We're flying Clinton!

CLINTON. Holy shit! Barely missed the rail there!

ERNIE-BOBO. Ahhhhhhh!

CLINTON. Screw the seat belts man. At this speed, it don't matter!

ERNIE-BOBO. It don't matter!

CLINTON. How much further?

ERNIE-BOBO. I don't know!

CLINTON. Where are we? Check the sign!

ERNIE-BOBO. Okay!

CLINTON. What's it say!

ERNIE-BOBO. GERMANY!

CLINTON. Fuck! *(Short pause.)* You always fuck it up.

ERNIE-BOBO. GERMANY!

CLINTON. Shut up you retard. Germany's not on the way to Mexico.

ERNIE-BOBO. Sorry.

CLINTON. Get out.

ERNIE-BOBO. Sorry Clinton.

CLINTON. Just — christ. Get out.

(Quick shift: As the lights fall on the car, lights rise on The Girl. She sits on the floor. Linda enters. Searches.)

LINDA. Jesus Christ.

THE GIRL. What?

LINDA. Nothing. *(Linda exits. Offstage:)* Christ.

THE GIRL. What are you looking for? *(Linda enters. Searches.)*

LINDA. Nothing. I'm late.

THE GIRL. Who is it?

LINDA. What?

THE GIRL. Tonight. Who?

LINDA. Michael.

THE GIRL. Oh.

LINDA. What?

THE GIRL. What?

LINDA. I say Michael, you say oh.

THE GIRL. Nothing.

LINDA. Okay. *(Linda searches.)*

THE GIRL. I don't like him.

LINDA. Well you don't have to go out with him.

THE GIRL. He smells weird. *(Linda exits. Reenters. Searches.)* Michael smells.

LINDA. He does not.

THE GIRL. He does. Like rubber. And he does that hair thing.

LINDA. Some men are very self-conscious about their hair.

THE GIRL. He's not fooling anyone.

LINDA. I know. *(Linda exits. Enters. Searches.)*

THE GIRL. But you like him? Michael?

LINDA. Sure. He's fine. He's very nice to me. We go places.

THE GIRL. But he's gross.

LINDA. Stop.

THE GIRL. You're a lot more attractive than him.

LINDA. Dammit.

THE GIRL. Mom.

LINDA. What? I'm sorry sweetie. What did you say?

THE GIRL. He takes you nice places because he knows you're prettiest he's ever going to get. He knows he's gross.

LINDA. He's got a good job.

THE GIRL. He works at the airport. Big deal.

LINDA. He's an air traffic controller.

THE GIRL. So?

LINDA. They make a lot of money.

THE GIRL. All the money in the world won't make him attractive.

LINDA. It can't hurt. *(Linda exits. Enters.)*

THE GIRL. We're fine. We don't need his money Mom. We're fine.

LINDA. Honey, did you see a little black box. Like this big.

THE GIRL. No.

LINDA. In my bathroom. Did you go in my bathroom?

THE GIRL. No.

LINDA. Shit.

THE GIRL. What?

LINDA. Nothing. Damn. That's that I guess.

THE GIRL. They get lost.

LINDA. What?

THE GIRL. They get lost sometimes.

LINDA. What does?

THE GIRL. Black boxes.

(Lights rise on Clinton and Jill. He sits at a table eating. She stares out the window.)

RAY. He shoved me hard into the grass

and slapped me in my face

This was in the summer of infinite heat

after they closed the beach front

after the Arabs took the oil away

when they razed the hillside

JILL. See how they do it. They grate it. They cut it into the hill. Put in ditches.

CLINTON. It looks like a cake.

JILL. Cul-de-sacs. They cut it in. Another week, they put the models up. And that's that.

CLINTON. They already did it.

JILL. No.

CLINTON. Other side of the hill. Ray went.

JILL. Ray who? Across the street Ray?

CLINTON. Yeah.

JILL. Why?

CLINTON. Just to see.

JILL. Is he buying?

CLINTON. Of course not. He just went to price it.

JILL. Price what?

CLINTON. You know, he went to compare.

JILL. They're selling?

CLINTON. His mom's sick.

JILL. I know that. Very sad.

CLINTON. He's gonna have to sell it. He just went to see what theirs is worth.

JILL. Theirs is worth four hundred.

CLINTON. He says five.

JILL. Oh please.

CLINTON. I don't know. I'm just telling you what he said.

JILL. Five hundred? He said five?

CLINTON. I guess.

JILL. That's ridiculous. He's just a boy. He has no idea what things cost.

CLINTON. He got pictures. Showed his mom. She knows about real estate.

JILL. What does she know?

CLINTON. She's smart.

JILL. No. Angela? Mrs. Wallace?

CLINTON. Dr. Wallace.

JILL. Oh please. She's a chiropractor Clinton.

CLINTON. So?

JILL. So that's like being a witch doctor.

CLINTON. No it's not.

JILL. Or a podiatrist or something. It's the same thing.

CLINTON. No it's not.

JILL. It is. You don't even have to go to college. She has no expertise.

CLINTON. She did good for herself.

JILL. What does that mean?

CLINTON. What?

JILL. She did good for herself. What do you mean by that?

CLINTON. Nothing. Just that she did good.

JILL. Did she?

CLINTON. You know, for her and Ray. She made money at her thing. She did good.

JILL. She did *well.* Are you defending her because she's sick?

CLINTON. I'm not defending anybody.

JILL. You say it like it's some special thing.

CLINTON. Her husband died.

JILL. So?

CLINTON. Forget it.

JILL. A single mother. Oh my. What an achievement.

CLINTON. Forget it okay. *(Pause.)*

JILL. She said five?

CLINTON. I don't know. That's what Ray said she said.

JILL. Poor woman. She's losing her mind. They have Model Three?

CLINTON. What?

JILL. They have Model Three?

CLINTON. I guess. Yeah.

JILL. They have an obstructed view.

CLINTON. No they don't.

JILL. It's obstructed. Everything on that side of the street is obstructed. They have less than ninety degrees. They have the trees from the school. It's obstructed.

CLINTON. Whatever.

JILL. Not whatever. It's audacious. Some people put on airs. It's disgusting. Five hundred? A half a million dollars? She wouldn't get a penny over four and she knows it. She calls herself a doctor. She tries to exert herself. Do you see what I'm saying?

CLINTON. No.

JILL. The Harris' got out right. 1976. And they got five and a half.

CLINTON. Fine.

JILL. And they had a pool.

CLINTON. May I be excused?

JILL. You know, you can walk this whole street and every other house has a single mother in it trying to raise a family. It's like a god-damned factory town or something. Like one of those places where they close the factory and all the men go away.

CLINTON. I know.

JILL. Which is harder? The one that dies, or the one that leaves for a stewardess.

CLINTON. Travel agent.

JILL. It's the same thing. Christ. Listen to me. I'm getting a migraine Clinton.

CLINTON. You want to lie down?

JILL. What?

CLINTON. A nap. You need to relax.

JILL. No. I can't. I have too much to do.

CLINTON. Like what?

JILL. You think I'm not busy enough?

CLINTON. No.

JILL. I work my ass off Clinton. Where's your job?

CLINTON. Forget it.

JILL. Look. Could you just get me an aspirin or something.

CLINTON. Sure.

JILL. Two. Please. *(Clinton exits. Jill looks out the window. Clinton reenters with a glass of water.)* She said five?

CLINTON. Don't get yourself worked up.

JILL. Can you imagine?

CLINTON. They have a city lights view.

JILL. What?

CLINTON. Relax.

JILL. They have a what?

CLINTON. City lights. You know, they can see the city and other people can see the hill.

JILL. Other people? Other people like us?

13

CLINTON. It's not a big deal.

JILL. Well apparently it is. Apparently a bunch of shitty lights are worth half a million dollars.

CLINTON. What do you care?

JILL. I care Clinton because I don't like having my family maligned.

CLINTON. What's wrong with you? No one's talking family. Jesus. We're talking real estate. A house.

JILL. A house is a family. A house is a family because they own it. The family owns. They live in the house. And let me tell you something about real estate Clinton. It's not worth what it's worth. It's not. It's worth what people say it's worth.

CLINTON. Mom —

JILL. When we bought this house, it was the highest on the hill. We were kings. They'll cut the cul-de-sacs up there. They'll pour the foundations. The Asians will move in —

CLINTON. Mom —

JILL. They'll be kings.

(Quick shift: Lights rise on Angela. Early evening. She looks out.)

RAY. He pinned my arms beneath his knees

and gathered a wad of phlegm in his throat

This was in the summer of infinite heat

When everything burned *(Ray-Ray brings her a tray of food.)*

ANGELA. You said, right back.

RAY-RAY. I burned it.

ANGELA. I remember. You said, right back. And I said, okay.

RAY-RAY. I burned it the first time. I let it get too hot.

ANGELA. Too hot.

RAY-RAY. It's okay now. I did it again. Brown. Not black. See?

ANGELA. It's brown.

RAY-RAY. I'm getting good. Remember when I used to burn it every time?

ANGELA. No.

RAY-RAY. Anyway, I'm faster now. I'm quick. My mind keeps the time. I know when to flip it now.

ANGELA. Okay. *(Short pause.)*

RAY-RAY. What are you looking at?

ANGELA. A flower.

RAY-RAY. A flower?

ANGELA. A flower. A spider. A bird.

RAY-RAY. That's good. I can get your paints. You can paint them later, if you want.

14

ANGELA. It's getting dark.

RAY-RAY. If you want. When you're done.

ANGELA. Okay.

RAY-RAY. You want this over there?

ANGELA. The bird likes the flower. The spider wants to eat the bird.

RAY-RAY. They don't eat birds.

ANGELA. Yes they do.

RAY-RAY. Sit up. How's a spider gonna catch a bird?

ANGELA. Birds fly. They dream most of the time. They don't think of spiders.

RAY-RAY. I guess.

ANGELA. Spiders think of nothing but birds.

RAY-RAY. You want salt?

ANGELA. The special salt.

RAY-RAY. That's right. *(Angela sits in front of the tray and considers the food. A short pause.)*

ANGELA. It's special.

RAY-RAY. Don't be a smart ass.

ANGELA. Sorry.

RAY-RAY. Well?

ANGELA. I'm waiting.

RAY-RAY. For what?

ANGELA. I don't know.

RAY-RAY. I'm very patient. Do you remember how patient I am?

ANGELA. No.

RAY-RAY. Very. More than you. I can stay here all night.

ANGELA. I'm not hungry.

RAY-RAY. Yes you are.

ANGELA. I'm not. There's no room inside me.

RAY-RAY. There's room for the carrots.

ANGELA. No.

RAY-RAY. One carrot.

ANGELA. I can't.

RAY-RAY. We're not going to do this.

ANGELA. No.

RAY-RAY. Please.

ANGELA. No.

RAY-RAY. String beans.

ANGELA. No.

RAY-RAY. One. One bean.

ANGELA. You say one, but it's never one.

15

RAY-RAY. We start with one.

ANGELA. No.

RAY-RAY. God Dammit.

ANGELA. I want to. I know what it means. To you. I know that. You make it. You try very hard. I know that.

RAY-RAY. Jesus —

ANGELA. It won't fit.

RAY-RAY. One bean.

ANGELA. No.

RAY-RAY. Here. *(He forks a bean.)* Here. Eat.

ANGELA. I can't make it fit if it won't. I can't force it.

RAY-RAY. I'll help you.

ANGELA. No.

RAY-RAY. Would you please just eat a friggin' bean?

ANGELA. I can't.

RAY-RAY. Jesus. *(Ray-Ray goes to the window and looks out.)* I don't know what to do. You know that, right? I'm not a professional.

ANGELA. I think I could maybe do the applesauce.

RAY-RAY. Okay. *(A short pause. Ray-Ray looks to Angela. She takes a bite.)*

ANGELA. Mmmmm.

RAY-RAY. Smart ass.

ANGELA. Apples are good.

RAY-RAY. A tarantula maybe. I bet a tarantula could eat a bird. They eat mice ... I don't see it.

ANGELA. He's there.

RAY-RAY. He must have moved on. Greener pastures.

ANGELA. He never moves.

RAY-RAY. Well I don't see him.

ANGELA. Across the street.

RAY-RAY. You can't see a spider across a street.

ANGELA. I can.

RAY-RAY. Where?

ANGELA. It's strange. My eyesight is getting better. Every day it gets better. I see things clearly now. Not just the thing. The thing inside the thing. Does that make sense?

RAY-RAY. No.

ANGELA. It's like x-ray vision. Maybe it's part of changing. I'm becoming something else. Like a super-hero or something. Soon I'll see everything perfectly.

RAY-RAY. Like a spider across a street.

16

ANGELA. That's right.

RAY-RAY. I don't believe you.

ANGELA. He's there.

RAY-RAY. Where?

ANGELA. In the garage.

RAY-RAY. Where?

ANGELA. On the car.

RAY-RAY. Are you kidding me?

ANGELA. He's right there. He's got a blue T-shirt on for Christ sake. I can't help you if you can't see that. *(Pause.)* What's wrong?

RAY-RAY. Nothing.

ANGELA. Did I say something wrong? I said something wrong, didn't I?

RAY-RAY. Blue T-shirt.

ANGELA. That's right.

RAY-RAY. That's Clinton. That's not a spider.

ANGELA. Hmm.

RAY-RAY. You know that.

ANGELA. I do?

RAY-RAY. You get confused sometimes. You get confused about words.

ANGELA. I say the wrong things.

RAY-RAY. It's okay.

ANGELA. I know they're wrong when I say them. They seem right. I see it. I give it a name. I say it.

RAY-RAY. It's all right.

ANGELA. I mix up the names of things. I see the spider in a blue T-shirt. I see the flower. She dyed her hair. I see the bird —

RAY-RAY. Stop.

ANGELA. And I don't remember much of anything anymore. I only remember that I once remembered something. The past is leaving. It gets replaced by something else. I don't know what it is. It's in my head now.

RAY-RAY. It's okay.

ANGELA. It scares you. It came up my throat. It traveled in my blood and dripped into my brain.

RAY-RAY. We'll go to the doctor.

ANGELA. They'll just tell us what we know.

RAY-RAY. I'm not scared. Don't be scared.

ANGELA. You're my son?

RAY-RAY. What?

ANGELA. I know that. I just don't remember how you got this way.

RAY-RAY. What way?

ANGELA. Like a man. I remember you when you were small. I remember that. You sucked on a sponge filled with ammonia. I remember being frightened. Frightened more than ever. More than now. I remember the hospital. The doctor. I screamed at him. He laughed. He gave you apple juice.

RAY-RAY. I know.

ANGELA. Apple juice. Because of acids and bases. Can you believe that? Sometimes apples have more power than death. You drank it. You lived.

RAY-RAY. I know. You told me.

ANGELA. Oh. I don't remember telling you.

RAY-RAY. It's okay.

ANGELA. I'm sorry. I'm so sorry.

RAY-RAY. It's okay.

ANGELA. I'm so sorry. I don't know what's happening.

RAY-RAY. Shhh. It's okay.

ANGELA. I don't know your name.

(Lights up on Clinton and The Girl.)

CLINTON. Are you staying?

THE GIRL. Do you want me to?

CLINTON. Do you want to?

THE GIRL. I don't know.

CLINTON. Stay. Where else you gonna go?

THE GIRL. I don't know.

CLINTON. You want to go upstairs?

THE GIRL. No. *(Short pause.)*

CLINTON. I'm gonna work on the car. You can stay if you want. *(He gets a tool box from upstage, opens it, and lies down on the mechanic's trolley.)*

THE GIRL. I saw your mom today Clinton. I saw her and she saw me.

CLINTON. So.

THE GIRL. So she looks at me funny.

CLINTON. She looks at everybody funny. *(He slides under the car.)*

THE GIRL. She looks at me like she can't figure me out — Like I'm something strange, you know?

CLINTON. No.

THE GIRL. I get all cold.

CLINTON. Are you pissed off or something?

18

THE GIRL. No.

CLINTON. If you're pissed off, you should go. No offense, but I can't deal with some kind of episode now.

THE GIRL. I'm not pissed off.

CLINTON. Okay.

THE GIRL. I'm just trying to talk to you.

CLINTON. So talk.

THE GIRL. She doesn't like me.

CLINTON. Come on.

THE GIRL. She doesn't. She thinks I'm a freak.

CLINTON. She likes you.

THE GIRL. Do you ever talk to her about me?

CLINTON. Give me a hand here.

THE GIRL. Clinton.

CLINTON. What?

THE GIRL. Do you ever talk to her about me?

CLINTON. Sure.

THE GIRL. What do you say?

CLINTON. I don't know. I say whatever she asks.

THE GIRL. Like what?

CLINTON. You know, whatever. I say I saw you. Or we hung out. I say I hang out with you sometimes.

THE GIRL. What does that mean?

CLINTON. It means we hang out.

THE GIRL. Jesus.

CLINTON. What?

THE GIRL. You're a fucking bastard, you know that? *(He slides out.)*

CLINTON. What's wrong with you?

THE GIRL. That lady thinks I'm dirt. She thinks I'm some kind of slut because I hang around here like a slut.

CLINTON. Don't get mental.

THE GIRL. You treat me like a slut Clinton.

CLINTON. I do not.

THE GIRL. You do. It's the same with Kilo and Ray-Ray. You don't even talk to me when they're around. You act like I don't exist —

CLINTON. Hold on —

THE GIRL. She probably thinks I'm fucking all of you. She looks at me like I'm some sort of slut. Or like she doesn't even know what I am. What am I?

CLINTON. What?

THE GIRL. What am I?

19

CLINTON. What does that mean? You're talking fucking non-sense. *(He slides under the car.)*

THE GIRL. What am I? To you.

CLINTON. What are you?

THE GIRL. To you.

CLINTON. You're like … You're like someone I hang out with. We do things.

THE GIRL. Oh, that's great.

CLINTON. What?

THE GIRL. I'm a slut.

CLINTON. Would you stop saying that?

THE GIRL. Does she know my name?

CLINTON. Yeah. She knows. Of course she knows.

THE GIRL. Did you tell her?

CLINTON. Did I tell her what?

THE GIRL. My name.

CLINTON. I don't have to tell her your name. She knows your name.

THE GIRL. How? She never introduced herself to me. I've been in this garage since the sixth grade, and not once has she offered her hand.

CLINTON. She knows I don't like her talking to my friends.

THE GIRL. Yeah. *(He slides out.)*

CLINTON. Are you on the rag?

THE GIRL. No Clinton, I'm not on the fucking rag.

CLINTON. Then why are you mental? You're wacked out. You been hacking on me all day. I don't like it.

THE GIRL. Tough shit.

CLINTON. Jesus.

THE GIRL. Do you dream of me?

CLINTON. What?

THE GIRL. Do you dream about me?

CLINTON. No. *(He slides under the car.)*

THE GIRL. Oh.

CLINTON. I don't dream.

THE GIRL. Figures.

CLINTON. I used to. Now. I just sleep. I get nothing. Blackness.

THE GIRL. I dream.

CLINTON. When I was a kid, I used to dream all sorts of things.

THE GIRL. I dream of you.

CLINTON. You shouldn't do that.

20

THE GIRL. Why not?

CLINTON. You just shouldn't.

THE GIRL. When I lay next to you. When you lie next to somebody and you're naked, and you're touching, your dreams mix. It's true. They bleed together.

CLINTON. I don't dream.

THE GIRL. You do. You just don't remember. I remember. I held your hand last night and your dreams melted into mine. That's what sex is, you know. You shoot your dreams inside me.

CLINTON. Knock it off.

THE GIRL. And mine leaked into you. Just dribbled down my finger and went inside. So my dreams are really your dreams. And yours are mine. *(He slides out.)*

CLINTON. I don't remember your dreams either. Hand me that.

THE GIRL. It's okay. You will.

CLINTON. Maybe your dreams aren't memorable.

THE GIRL. That's a shitty thing to say.

CLINTON. I guess.

THE GIRL. You're mean. Why are you mean to me?

CLINTON. I don't know. You make me nervous.

THE GIRL. Well, I guess that's something.

CLINTON. Wrench.

THE GIRL. Which?

CLINTON. Three-eighths. *(She hands it to him. Clinton slides back under the car. The Girl looks at him. Pause.)*

THE GIRL. It makes me hot sometimes.

CLINTON. What?

THE GIRL. It makes me hot. *(Clinton slides out.)*

CLINTON. What does?

THE GIRL. When you're mean.

CLINTON. When I'm mean?

THE GIRL. I know. It's not healthy. I shouldn't come here.

CLINTON. But you do.

THE GIRL. Yeah.

CLINTON. It makes you hot.

THE GIRL. Yeah.

CLINTON. I can be pretty mean.

THE GIRL. Let's stop.

CLINTON. I can be downright evil sometimes.

THE GIRL. I could cure you.

CLINTON. Somebody should. I can be pretty ill-behaved.

21

THE GIRL. I could take you upstairs and let you shoot it all up in me. Then you wouldn't have it no more. It would be mine.

CLINTON. It doesn't work like that.

THE GIRL. Maybe it does.

CLINTON. It doesn't travel.

THE GIRL. How would you know?

CLINTON. 'Cause I'm not crazy. *(Clinton grabs a screwdriver and slides back under.)*

THE GIRL. That's how it works.

CLINTON. Shut up, okay.

THE GIRL. Why do you think you cry when you cum? *(Clinton slides out.)*

CLINTON. Shut up.

THE GIRL. Cry baby.

CLINTON. I could stick this in your eye.

THE GIRL. So stick me.

CLINTON. You never grow up.

THE GIRL. Stick me with your screwdriver Clinton.

CLINTON. Go home.

THE GIRL. It's not a school night. *(Short pause.)* Cry baby. *(He rushes The Girl and pins her to the car. He presses the tip of the screwdriver to her neck. She sticks her tongue out at him. A beat. They begin to make out, eyes open, desperate, clumsy. Clinton trails the screwdriver slowly down her torso and pushes it between her legs.)* I like it when you make it like the movies.

CLINTON. Don't talk.

THE GIRL. Is your mom home?

CLINTON. Yeah.

THE GIRL. Wait.

CLINTON. We'll be quiet.

THE GIRL. Wait. Wait.

CLINTON. Shhh.

THE GIRL. Wait!

CLINTON. What?

THE GIRL. I gotta do my thing.

CLINTON. You don't got it in?

THE GIRL. What are you, nuts? You don't walk around with it up there.

CLINTON. Oh.

THE GIRL. It's not a tampon, stupid.

CLINTON. I don't know.

22

THE GIRL. Jesus. I need a bathroom.

CLINTON. So go.

THE GIRL. I'm not going in there.

CLINTON. Why not? She doesn't know anything.

THE GIRL. Is that what you think?

CLINTON. Go to Ray-Ray's.

THE GIRL. Oh fuck off.

CLINTON. Right across the street. Right there.

THE GIRL. I'm not going over there.

CLINTON. Why?

THE GIRL. 'Cause it's not right.

CLINTON. What are you talking about? Just go.

THE GIRL. You don't go into a dying lady's house to stick things in your whatnot.

CLINTON. Is that a rule?

THE GIRL. It's called morals.

CLINTON. Jesus.

THE GIRL. Here. Hold this. *(The Girl opens her purse and takes out a small black box. She hands the purse to Clinton.)* Keep a lookout. *(The Girl goes behind the car and crouches.)*

CLINTON. Your thing is complicated.

THE GIRL. I beg your pardon.

CLINTON. Got preparations like Thanksgiving. *(To offstage:)* What up Ray-Ray. *(Ray-Ray enters.)*

RAY-RAY. I got to talk with you.

CLINTON. Oh yeah?

RAY-RAY. Serious yo. We got an issue.

CLINTON. Speak like a white person.

RAY-RAY. Can we talk?

CLINTON. Kinda busy here.

RAY-RAY. It's important.

CLINTON. I'll yell for you later.

RAY-RAY. Why The Girl behind the car?

CLINTON. What's that?

RAY-RAY. Girl!

CLINTON. She's helping me.

RAY-RAY. Girl, what you think you doing?

THE GIRL. I'm helping Clinton.

RAY-RAY. Helping Clinton what?

THE GIRL. With the car.

RAY-RAY. You don't know shit about cars.

CLINTON. She's learning.

RAY-RAY. She's fourteen Clinton.

CLINTON. So?

RAY-RAY. So she's fourteen and you're nineteen.

CLINTON. What are you trying to say?

RAY-RAY. I'm just trying to say she's fourteen.

CLINTON. What do you want Raymond?

RAY-RAY. You know that ain't my name.

CLINTON. What do you want?

RAY-RAY. You shit bag my house?

CLINTON. I beg your pardon.

RAY-RAY. Did you shit in a bag and throw it at my house?

CLINTON. Me?

RAY-RAY. Yeah, you.

CLINTON. Are you trying to piss me off?

RAY-RAY. I'm trying to figure out if you shit-bagged my mom's house.

CLINTON. And if I did?

RAY-RAY. I guess we got a problem then.

CLINTON. That so?

RAY-RAY. Did you do it?

CLINTON. What are you doing here Ray?

RAY-RAY. Do what I have to.

THE GIRL. Ray-Ray —

CLINTON. Let him talk. Hypothetically, if I did, what would you do Raymond? Would you kick my ass?

RAY-RAY. I guess.

CLINTON. You guess? That doesn't sound like a real ass-kicking thing to say. Either you're gonna kick my ass or you're not. Which is it? Or maybe I should kick your ass seeing as you accused me and all.

THE GIRL. Nobody's accusing.

CLINTON. I don't think that's true. Is it Raymond? Are you accusing me of throwing human feces on your mommy's house?

RAY-RAY. Yes.

THE GIRL. Go home Ray-Ray.

CLINTON. I guess we do have a problem.

RAY-RAY. Did you do it?

CLINTON. Tell you what. I'm feeling very fucking hurt here Ray. But I'm going to let you slide seeing as your Mom's all cancerous and what-not.

RAY-RAY. You don't say shit about my Mom.

CLINTON. I'm just stating the facts here.

RAY-RAY. Take it back.

CLINTON. Relax. Look at you. You're upset. Girl, tell him to relax.

RAY-RAY. Did you do it?

CLINTON. What makes you think I did it?

RAY-RAY. How many times I watch you do it Clinton? How many times you shit-bag somebody?

CLINTON. That was junior high. It's a kid trick.

RAY-RAY. We ain't kids no more.

THE GIRL. Boys.

CLINTON. Come here.

RAY-RAY. You break everything Clinton.

CLINTON. Come over here Ray-Ray.

RAY-RAY. I ain't afraid to fight you.

CLINTON. We're not gonna fight.

RAY-RAY. You got your fight face on.

CLINTON. No.

THE GIRL. Stop it. Go home Ray-Ray.

RAY-RAY. Your eyes are tight. Like slits.

CLINTON. I'm just looking at you.

RAY-RAY. I know the face Clinton. How many times you think I seen that face.

CLINTON. Lots.

RAY-RAY. Lots and lots. Your eyes get tight. Then you swing.

CLINTON. I'm not gonna swing.

RAY-RAY. Then you thinking about swinging.

CLINTON. No.

RAY-RAY. You are. You can't hide it from me. I grew up under your fists. I know the face.

CLINTON. This face means more than fists Ray-Ray.

RAY-RAY. That's funny 'cause every time I ever seen it, blood come out my nose.

CLINTON. Come here.

RAY-RAY. No.

CLINTON. You scared?

RAY-RAY. Maybe. Don't mean I won't scrap Clinton. I'll scrap with you.

CLINTON. I know.

RAY-RAY. You can smack my teeth on the driveway again. You can chip them all up again. I don't give a fuck.

CLINTON. Come here.

THE GIRL. Clinton. Don't.

RAY-RAY. I'm pretty far past the point of giving a fuck, you know?

CLINTON. Come here Ray-Ray.

RAY-RAY. Did you do it?

CLINTON. No.

RAY-RAY. I don't believe you.

CLINTON. Come on Raymond.

RAY-RAY. I ain't gonna cry this time. *(Clinton beats the crap out of Ray-Ray. They wind up down stage, Ray-Ray on his back. Clinton straddles Ray-Ray's chest, pinning his arms beneath his knees. Ray-Ray struggles.)*

CLINTON. You done?

RAY-RAY. GET OFF ME!

CLINTON. Relax.

RAY-RAY. Get off me motherfucker!

CLINTON. Easy.

THE GIRL. You're hurting him.

CLINTON. He wants it.

RAY-RAY. I hate you.

CLINTON. Okay.

RAY-RAY. I fucking hate you Clinton!

CLINTON. It's all right.

RAY-RAY. Why you mean Clinton? Why you mean to me?

CLINTON. 'Cause you don't have a Dad. 'Cause your mom is dying.

RAY-RAY. FUCK YOU!

CLINTON. 'Cause you were a soft little shit. You was soft, remember? The bike jump, remember?

RAY-RAY. Nobody shit bags my mom!

CLINTON. You jumped. You flipped over the bars. Your arm —

RAY-RAY. Nobody shit bags my mom!

CLINTON. You cried your little eyes out. You cried, remember?

RAY-RAY. Nobody! Fuck!

CLINTON. Who put the bone back in?

RAY-RAY. Fuck.

CLINTON. Who pushed it back in?

RAY-RAY. You.

CLINTON. That's right. I put it back. Same reason I chipped your teeth. Same reason I spit on you.

RAY-RAY. Fuck. Fuck.

CLINTON. You're not a boy anymore. You don't cry. You'll be a

26

man Ray-Ray. You'll be a man when she's dead.

RAY-RAY. Shut up.

CLINTON. When she's dead you won't cry. It'll hurt like a thousand bike jumps and you won't cry. You'll ache. In your shoulders. In your balls. You'll feel them for the first time. Because I gave them to you.

RAY-RAY. Did you do it?

CLINTON. No Raymond. I did not.

RAY-RAY. I'm alone.

CLINTON. You got me.

RAY-RAY. I got you.

CLINTON. That's right. Now I gotta mark you.

THE GIRL. No.

CLINTON. Come on Ray. Open up.

THE GIRL. Clinton don't.

CLINTON. You know the rules. Open your mouth … Open your fucking mouth Ray. *(He does. A beat. Clinton laughs.)* Don't flinch. *(Clinton clears his throat. He leans over Ray-Ray and spits into his mouth. Clinton gets off of Ray-Ray and sits on the car. Ray-Ray rises to his hands and knees. He spits. His nose bleeds.)* Get him a towel. *(The Girl takes a greasy towel from the hood of the car and goes to Ray-Ray.)*

THE GIRL. This is some twisted shit Clinton. You're fucking twisted.

CLINTON. Shut up.

RAY-RAY. Fuck.

CLINTON. You all right?

RAY-RAY. Yeah. *(Clinton exits.)*

THE GIRL. Fucking twisted macho crap. Here, lean back.

RAY-RAY. Fuck.

THE GIRL. Hey Ray-Ray. Can I use your bathroom? *(Lights down on The Girl.)*

RAY. In the summer of infinite heat
I was crucified
I lay squirming and screaming beneath the loogie
that dangled from one impossibly thin transparent thread
and clung to his sun-cracked lips
and he laughed
and it broke
something inside me.

ANGELA. What are you doing?

RAY-RAY. Nothing.

ANGELA. You've been there for an hour. I can see in the dark.

27

RAY-RAY. Are you okay?

ANGELA. I'm fine.

RAY-RAY. I was just checking on you.

ANGELA. You were listening to my breath.

RAY-RAY. I guess.

ANGELA. To see if it stopped.

RAY-RAY. No.

ANGELA. It's okay. I do it too. I hear the breath and then I wait. The wait is the hard part. It's hard to be certain. But it comes.

RAY-RAY. Do you want anything?

ANGELA. I'm always surprised when it comes.

RAY-RAY. We got apple juice.

ANGELA. No. No more apples.

RAY-RAY. Okay.

ANGELA. Come here. *(Ray-Ray flips on the light.)* Ohh. Turn it down. *(He dims the light.)* My eyes are very sensitive.

RAY-RAY. Sorry.

ANGELA. It's okay. Come here. *(Ray-Ray crosses to her.)* Don't look so sad.

RAY-RAY. I'm not.

ANGELA. Give me a smile. Hmm. That's nice. It makes it pretty.

RAY-RAY. Tell me what to do.

ANGELA. I don't know.

RAY-RAY. Please.

ANGELA. You could get my paints. *(Ray-Ray looks at her painting.)*

RAY-RAY. It's nice.

ANGELA. Thank you.

RAY-RAY. Is this a bird?

ANGELA. Yes.

RAY-RAY. And this is a spider.

ANGELA. No.

RAY-RAY. Oh.

ANGELA. That's another bird.

RAY-RAY. Oh.

ANGELA. It's okay. I know it's a bird. That's what matters.

RAY-RAY. Is this the spider?

ANGELA. Bird.

RAY-RAY. I thought you were painting a spider.

ANGELA. He's hard to paint.

RAY-RAY. He is?

ANGELA. Everything's a bird now.

RAY-RAY. Oh.

ANGELA. What's wrong?

RAY-RAY. Nothing.

ANGELA. Tell me what you're thinking.

RAY-RAY. You're almost finished.

ANGELA. Yes.

RAY-RAY. What do you want to do with it?

ANGELA. What do you mean?

RAY-RAY. Can I have it?

ANGELA. Of course. It's always been for you.

RAY-RAY. I don't want you to go.

ANGELA. When you sell the house, don't let them fix the concrete. The part we put our hands in. That stays.

RAY-RAY. I can't do anything about that.

ANGELA. It stays.

RAY-RAY. I'll try.

ANGELA. I used to look at it when I was gardening. The imprints. Your tiny hands. My hands. Your father's. He had gigantic hands.

RAY-RAY. I know.

ANGELA. He had a big penis.

RAY-RAY. Mom!

ANGELA. Sorry. I think about him a lot now.

RAY-RAY. Jesus.

ANGELA. Don't be so uptight. Every son should know about his father.

RAY-RAY. Not his dick.

ANGELA. Especially his dick … God … I'm funny. I'm funny now. I was never funny, was I?

RAY-RAY. Sure. You were funny.

ANGELA. Not like this. It improves one's sense of humor. Here give me those. *(Ray-Ray hands her the tray of paints. She dips her brush in the black paint.)* Sit. *(Ray-Ray sits. Angela reaches out with the brush.)*

RAY-RAY. What are you doing?

ANGELA. It's okay. Relax.

RAY-RAY. Don't.

ANGELA. Hold still.

RAY-RAY. It's not Halloween.

ANGELA. Please. *(She touches the brush to Ray-Ray's cheek.)*

RAY-RAY. What are you doing? *(Angela laughs. She paints his face.)* Mom.

29

ANGELA. See? *(Ray-Ray looks at his reflection in the window.)*
RAY-RAY. What's this?
ANGELA. Do you see? We match. We'll look grand.
RAY-RAY. What is this?
ANGELA. It's your death face. *(Blackout.)*

ACT TWO

Lights up on Ray.

RAY. There was only one season
There was only sun
No change in weather marked the passage of time
There was no time
Only sun
Forever sun
At night, I sat death-quiet in the shadow of the window
Pit viper under a rock
I felt his heat in the hollow of my ears
and waited for his light to come on
It was the season of St. Helen's
It was the season of shedding skin *(Lights up on The Girl and Linda, sitting on the floor. They've been trading pedicures. Linda paints The Girl's toes. A pause.)*
THE GIRL. What's a rim job?
LINDA. What?
THE GIRL. Never mind.
LINDA. Where did you hear that?
THE GIRL. I didn't.
LINDA. You did. You just said it. Did somebody say that to you?
THE GIRL. No. *(Short pause.)*
LINDA. You don't know what it is?
THE GIRL. I know.
LINDA. My God.
THE GIRL. Forget it.
LINDA. You asked. You don't know.
THE GIRL. I wanted to see if you knew.
LINDA. Oh. I know.
THE GIRL. Then what is it?
LINDA. Look, I don't need my vocabulary tested here. I'm your mother.
THE GIRL. So?

LINDA. So I know more words than you. I'm older.

THE GIRL. That doesn't mean anything.

LINDA. I have twenty more years of words. That's what that means.

THE GIRL. Then what is it?

LINDA. I … Do you want to talk about this? If you want to talk about this, we can … Who said that to you?

THE GIRL. Nobody, I told you.

LINDA. That's … God … That's really not appropriate.

THE GIRL. Oh please.

LINDA. You shouldn't say things like that. You're too young.

THE GIRL. It's bad.

LINDA. Where did you hear that?

THE GIRL. Is it bad or good?

LINDA. I thought you knew.

THE GIRL. I do.

LINDA. Then you know. You can tell yourself.

THE GIRL. Forget it. I'll ask somebody else.

LINDA. Don't do that.

THE GIRL. Why?

LINDA. You just shouldn't say it. It's better if you don't know. You don't want to get a reputation.

THE GIRL. You don't get a reputation from a word.

LINDA. You don't know how men think.

THE GIRL. Yes I do.

LINDA. You have no idea.

THE GIRL. I know lots of guys.

LINDA. So do I.

THE GIRL. I don't have a reputation. Do you think I have a reputation?

LINDA. I don't know. Maybe it rubbed off on you.

THE GIRL. What?

LINDA. I'm not married, you know? People talk. Maybe some of it gets on you.

THE GIRL. I'm not a slut Mom.

LINDA. I'm just saying. A word can get on your skin. *(Pause.)*

THE GIRL. It got on the wall too.

LINDA. What?

THE GIRL. In the boys' room. Somebody wrote it.

LINDA. What?

THE GIRL. "The Girl gives rim-jobs." They wrote that. And all these guys signed their names under it. Like I did that to them. But

I didn't. I swear to God. I never did.

(Lights up on Clinton and Jill. She smokes.)

CLINTON. How long have you been standing there?

JILL. I don't know. It was lighter. I don't know.

CLINTON. Have you been drinking?

JILL. I am allowed.

CLINTON. Is this what you did all day?

JILL. No. This is not what I did all day.

CLINTON. What did you do?

JILL. I don't have to account for my time.

CLINTON. I left. You were still in bed.

JILL. I got a late start.

CLINTON. You stay up all night.

JILL. Don't exaggerate.

CLINTON. What did you do today? Did you go to work?

JILL. I did lots of things. You're not aware of everything I do.

CLINTON. Like what?

JILL. I don't like your tone.

CLINTON. Never mind.

JILL. I walked the dog. We walked.

CLINTON. You're going to get fired.

JILL. We don't need the money. Don't worry.

CLINTON. I worry.

JILL. What have you got to worry about?

CLINTON. You.

JILL. Me?

CLINTON. Yes.

JILL. That's ridiculous.

CLINTON. Forget it.

JILL. No. I like it. It's very sweet.

CLINTON. I'm going to bed.

JILL. Give me a kiss. *(He does.)* You know, when I first saw you — the very first time I laid eyes on you, I couldn't believe how small you were. You were very, very small you see. Because I smoked.

CLINTON. Oh.

JILL. Do you forgive me?

CLINTON. Sure. They didn't know then what they know now.

JILL. No, they knew. I just couldn't help myself. I'm terrible.

CLINTON. It's okay.

JILL. You forgive me?

CLINTON. Yeah.

JILL. Say it.

CLINTON. I forgive you.

JILL. Come closer. I can't see your eyes. *(He moves closer. She touches his hair.)* You have such pretty eyes. They're the first thing I remember. I looked at you. Little pink face. Little hands. And I think — I thought you were the very best of me. I thought you were going to make me worth something.

CLINTON. Mom —

JILL. What happened?

CLINTON. What?

JILL. Everything was going so well.

CLINTON. When?

JILL. Before. I was happy. He was … We had potential. We had the potential to be happy. Were you happy?

CLINTON. When?

JILL. Before.

CLINTON. I don't know.

JILL. You were happy. How could you not have been.

CLINTON. You shouldn't drink.

JILL. A nice house. A nice school. A mother to make you sandwiches. A father to take you to ball games.

CLINTON. Mom —

JILL. That's how it was. Do you remember?

CLINTON. No.

JILL. Of course you do. You and he wore your hats. Matching hats. With the little L-A on the front. I made you sandwiches.

CLINTON. Mom —

JILL. A picnic. And you and he got in the car. I remember you waving from the window. My good men. Going to the ball game. That's how it was. Do you remember?

CLINTON. Yes.

JILL. So many summers. So many games.

CLINTON. One.

JILL. What?

CLINTON. One game. We went once.

JILL. No.

CLINTON. Yes.

JILL. No. I remember.

CLINTON. One game. They played the Padres. Fernando pitched.

JILL. No.

CLINTON. Ron Sey hit a two-run homer in the eighth.

JILL. There were many games.

CLINTON. One game.

JILL. No. I remember. Don't you think I'd remember something like that?

CLINTON. You're tired.

JILL. There were many games. You were too young.

CLINTON. That's not true.

JILL. Don't you tell me what's true and not true. Don't contradict me Clinton. I know what's true. I remember. I remember it that way because that's the way it was. And he loved us. And that's how it was. Exactly.

CLINTON. Look at me.

JILL. Why?

CLINTON. Are you going to cry?

JILL. Of course not.

CLINTON. I wish you would.

JILL. You'd like that wouldn't you. So hateful.

CLINTON. I didn't mean it like that.

JILL. You think I'm terrible. *(Clinton moves to leave.)* Where are you going?

CLINTON. I'm gonna go work on the car.

JILL. Ah yes. The car. The famous car. How long have you had that car Clinton?

CLINTON. I don't know.

JILL. You don't know because you don't want to say it out loud? Or, you don't know because it's been so long that you can't remember?

CLINTON. Two years.

JILL. I could have sworn it was longer than that.

CLINTON. Can I go?

JILL. Go where Clinton? You have no car. Your father left you a car and you — Do you remember?

CLINTON. What?

JILL. You were so eager. "I'm gonna fix it up Mom. I'm gonna fix it and drive down to Mexico." Do you remember?

CLINTON. I am going to fix it.

JILL. Of course you are. Of course. Do you remember what I said?

CLINTON. Yes.

JILL. What did I say?

CLINTON. I don't know.

JILL. I said you'd never get it done.

CLINTON. I'm leaving.

JILL. Sure. Go ahead. Go hide under the hood of that heap.

CLINTON. That's not what I meant.

JILL. What did you mean? *(Short pause.)* Am I so terrible? *(Short pause.)* You think I'm terrible.

CLINTON. No.

JILL. I'm terrible.

CLINTON. You're not terrible.

JILL. I say terrible things.

CLINTON. Stop.

JILL. I do them. I do terrible things Clinton.

CLINTON. No you don't.

JILL. I was walking the dog around the block. He did his thing. And I picked it up and threw it at her house.

CLINTON. What?

JILL. I threw shit on her house Clinton. On that dying woman's house.

CLINTON. You did what?

JILL. And I don't know why. I don't know why I did it.

(Lights up on Ray-Ray, sitting on the floor downstage, smoking a joint. Clinton works on the car.)

CLINTON. I love it like this. Right now.

RAY-RAY. I know.

CLINTON. Night. But hot as a motherfucker. I feel that little buzz. I feel the vibrations and shit. Do you feel that?

RAY-RAY. What?

CLINTON. Like … you want to run, or fuck something. Or kill it.

RAY-RAY. I don't know.

CLINTON. Sun goes down. Everything starts waking up. Nighttime things. Things that live in the ground. Snakes, spiders, coyotes … you think they still got coyotes?

RAY-RAY. I don't know.

CLINTON. I never hear them anymore. *(Short pause.)*

RAY-RAY. They still got snakes.

CLINTON. Yeah. Yes they do. 'Cause it's a desert. That's what it really is. Don't bogart that. *(Ray-Ray passes the jay to Clinton who takes a hit and passes it back.)* They landscape, you know. They irrigate. But it's a desert underneath. They have water flying out of sprinklers from some river a thousand miles away. It's a lie.

RAY-RAY. It tastes gummy.

CLINTON. Unlike Mexico, which is not a lie. Mexico is desert. Mexico exists.

RAY-RAY. Serious, it tastes gummy or something.

CLINTON. What the fuck is gummy?

RAY-RAY. I don't know.

CLINTON. Look at you. It's because it's good. You smoke all that high-school bullshit. You don't know what the good shit tastes like.

RAY-RAY. It tastes gummy.

CLINTON. Shut the fuck up. *(Pause. Clinton pops the car's hood. Ray-Ray continues looking at the hill.)* The openness. Mexico. Space and light. Like an ocean of land. Empty. Just going on forever and ever until it hits the ocean.

RAY-RAY. The water ocean.

CLINTON. Yeah ... the water ocean. And there's a beach. And it's perfect. No people. No fucking crap to deal with. Just the sand. And the waves. I'm going to Mexico.

RAY-RAY. Bullshit.

CLINTON. Fuck you bullshit.

RAY-RAY. You say that for years.

CLINTON. I'm waking up Ray. Look at my hands man. I'm shaking. *(Ray-Ray smokes.)*

RAY-RAY. Damn. They cut the shit out of that motherfucker. You see this? This is some fucked up shit Clinton. You should see this.

CLINTON. I've seen.

RAY-RAY. They tore the shit up. They do that yesterday?

CLINTON. What?

RAY-RAY. I didn't notice. I usually notice, you know, the change. It's slow. Like they do it one cul-de-sac at a time. Like I look up and bam. It got erased.

CLINTON. I'm shaking.

RAY-RAY. Guess I didn't look up yesterday. Guess I forgot to look up. *(Short pause.)*

CLINTON. It's mine anyway.

RAY-RAY. What?

CLINTON. It's mine.

RAY-RAY. What is?

CLINTON. The hill dumbass.

RAY-RAY. The hill?

CLINTON. Yeah.

RAY-RAY. Bullshit.

CLINTON. It is.

RAY-RAY. How you figure?

CLINTON. 'Cause I was a kid up there.

RAY-RAY. So was I.

CLINTON. I was a kid before you were. I used to go up there, kill rattlesnakes.

RAY-RAY. Bullshit. You never killed no snake.

CLINTON. Fuck you I fucking killed fucking rattlesnakes. I go up there. Gunnysack and a stick. Cut their heads off. Make a necklace out of the rattles.

RAY-RAY. Bullshit.

CLINTON. Are you calling me a liar?

RAY-RAY. No.

CLINTON. Don't call me a fucking liar.

RAY-RAY. You still got it?

CLINTON. What?

RAY-RAY. The rattles. The rattle necklace.

CLINTON. My mom threw it out.

RAY-RAY. Right.

CLINTON. Fuck you Ray. It's true. They used to call me the snake man.

RAY-RAY. Bullshit. Who called you that?

CLINTON. People.

RAY-RAY. What people?

CLINTON. People you don't know.

RAY-RAY. Oh.

CLINTON. Don't give me that look.

RAY-RAY. What look?

CLINTON. That look right there. Don't do that.

RAY-RAY. Relax.

CLINTON. Man … You got no idea. I'd creep up on them. Real slow. Get my bag in one hand. Real slow. Uncoil them with the stick. Slow. They don't even mind. *(Clinton creeps on Ray-Ray.)*

RAY-RAY. Clinton.

CLINTON. Get my hand ready. You have to get them the first time. You got to watch the neck. The base of the head. Slow.

RAY-RAY. Don't.

CLINTON. Don't move.

RAY-RAY. Come on.

CLINTON. You get as close as you can.

RAY-RAY. Clinton — *(Clinton's hand thrusts out and seizes the back of Ray-Ray's neck.)* FUCK! *(Ray-Ray tries to turn on Clinton. They wrestle. Eventually Clinton takes Ray-Ray to the dirt. Ray-Ray, on his hands and knees, struggles to get out. Clinton, puts him in a hold, his*

chest tight on Ray-Ray's back. His fingers press into Ray-Ray's pectoral.)
GET THE FUCK OFF!

CLINTON. Holy shit, what's this?

RAY-RAY. I don't want to do this.

CLINTON. What's this? Feel that shit. This is hard here.

RAY-RAY. My arms are numb.

CLINTON. I think you've been working out. I think you've been secretly training or some shit like that.

RAY-RAY. I'm serious Clinton.

CLINTON. 'Cause this is hard right here. *(Ray-Ray struggles again. Clinton contains him.)*

RAY-RAY. Clinton.

CLINTON. Bump-bum. Bump-bum.

RAY-RAY. Get off.

CLINTON. Shhhh …

RAY-RAY. I don't feel good.

CLINTON. Bump-bum. Bump-bum.

RAY-RAY. Stop.

CLINTON. That's your heart Ray.

RAY-RAY. I feel sick.

CLINTON. Listen. Bump-bum.

RAY-RAY. Please.

CLINTON. Can you feel mine? *(Ray-Ray goes wild. He tries to escape again. Clinton recovers control. Ray-Ray is exhausted.)*

RAY-RAY. Let go.

CLINTON. What's my name?

RAY-RAY. I'm gonna puke.

CLINTON. Don't puke.

RAY-RAY. Let go.

CLINTON. Say my name.

RAY-RAY. Clinton. *(Clinton tightens his hold.)* Ow. Fuck.

CLINTON. No. Who am I?

RAY-RAY. What? *(Tighter.)*

CLINTON. Who am I?

RAY-RAY. What? *(Tighter.)* Oww. Stop.

CLINTON. Say it. Who am I?

RAY-RAY. You're the snake man.

CLINTON. That's right Ray. I am the snake man and this is a perfect world. *(Blackout. In darkness:)*

ANGELA. RAYMOND! RAYMOND!

RAY-RAY. Mom! *(Lights up on Ray-Ray and Angela.)*

ANGELA. Raymond?

RAY-RAY. No Mom. It's me. It's Ray.

ANGELA. Who?

RAY-RAY. I'm here. It's all right.

ANGELA. Dreams. Terrible. I have dreams.

RAY-RAY. Shhhh.

ANGELA. I was a bird.

RAY-RAY. You're okay.

ANGELA. I was bird. I was a crow, in my nest. A dark place in the wood awnings. Of this house.

RAY-RAY. Shhh.

ANGELA. I had children. I fed them from my mouth. She laid her eggs on me. While I slept. I never knew. Black widows love wood awnings.

RAY-RAY. Stop.

ANGELA. They hatched when I flew. They hatched. They were eating me. Hundreds. Eating my feathers and skin. I was falling. They ate me. I fell.

RAY-RAY. Please.

ANGELA. When I hit the ground, I was only bone.

(Lights up on Clinton and The Girl.)

THE GIRL. It's some kind of ceremony and there's people. My mom's in the crowd. She looks all scared. And in the middle — it's like this big ring — like a what-do-you-call-it — like arena, and I'm getting led in by these big nameless-faceless guys. And there's this table. One of those nameless tables. Medical table. With the things for your legs. And they put me up there and strap me in. I got a white robe on. They strap me in and spread me. There's this doctor type guy. I see him. He's got a mask, you know. Like they have. And all of a sudden I get it. Like I thought it was fun or something before. Like it was a show. But it's not. He's got this thing. Like a long white thing with a handle and like a light on the end. He's gonna check me. And he checks me and turns around and all the lights change and get all red and everybody like gasps. All upset. My mom's all upset. Crying. And I'm crying. And the white thing. The checking thing starts growing in his hand, getting long and sharp. He walks towards me. I start screaming. I'm screaming that it happened riding horses. I'm screaming gymnastics. He shakes his head. Everybody knows it's a lie. I see you. I want you to tell them. I want you to stop them. I want you to say I didn't do it myself. I want you to save me. I'm screaming for you to save me. But you don't hear.

Or you do and you just ... I don't know.

CLINTON. Pay attention.

THE GIRL. What do you think of that?

CLINTON. What do I think of what?

THE GIRL. Jesus. What I said Clinton. What I just said to you.

CLINTON. I told you not to do that.

THE GIRL. I can't help what I dream Clinton.

CLINTON. I told you not to.

THE GIRL. Can we go outside?

CLINTON. No.

THE GIRL. Let's go to the garage. I don't like it in here.

CLINTON. You're not looking.

THE GIRL. Yes I am.

CLINTON. No. You're not.

THE GIRL. I'm looking. I got my eyes — Look. I'm looking.

CLINTON. What do see?

THE GIRL. The sunset.

CLINTON. You're not looking.

THE GIRL. I want to talk. Can we talk?

CLINTON. No.

THE GIRL. My heart hurts Clinton.

CLINTON. It's the smog.

THE GIRL. I gotta talk to somebody.

CLINTON. Wait.

THE GIRL. Clinton.

CLINTON. You're gonna miss it.

THE GIRL. Miss what?

CLINTON. Just look.

THE GIRL. Fuck this.

CLINTON. What do you see?

THE GIRL. I ... I don't know. What do you want me to see?

CLINTON. Nothing. Forget it.

THE GIRL. I see buildings. I see hills. I see ocean. I see airport. I see 5. I see 405. I see —

CLINTON. It's fire.

THE GIRL. What?

CLINTON. It's on fire.

THE GIRL. What is?

CLINTON. All of it. When it goes behind the buildings. It lights all the black glass. Lights it all up orange. Like all the glass is melting and orange. Like they nuked it.

THE GIRL. We gotta talk.

CLINTON. It's perfect. Do you see?

THE GIRL. Yes.

CLINTON. What do you see?

THE GIRL. Everything you said.

CLINTON. Bullshit.

THE GIRL. Why don't you listen to me?

CLINTON. 'Cause I don't listen when I look.

THE GIRL. Clinton —

CLINTON. Everything melts. Every piece of glass in every building. Every windshield. Every windshield on the freeway. It's a lava river. The freeway. I put my face on the glass — Put your face on the glass.

THE GIRL. What?

CLINTON. Put your face on the glass.

THE GIRL. Why?

CLINTON. It's flowing right into my mouth.

THE GIRL. I don't like it when you talk like this.

CLINTON. Then don't listen.

THE GIRL. Why can't you look at me?

CLINTON. I'm looking at the reflection. Look at the reflection. Put your face on the glass. *(She does.)* I used to imagine it was a lava river. See? And Palos Verdes was a big volcano. And this was somewhere else … Do you see it?

THE GIRL. The reflection?

CLINTON. Yeah.

THE GIRL. I just see you.

CLINTON. It's no good.

THE GIRL. Clinton.

CLINTON. It's no good. Go home.

THE GIRL. No.

CLINTON. I want to be alone.

THE GIRL. I gotta talk to somebody. I got nobody to talk to.

CLINTON. Go home Girl.

THE GIRL. I got nobody to —

CLINTON. GO HOME! *(She moves upstage to leave. Stops.)*

THE GIRL. Did you know they make diaphragms in different sizes?

CLINTON. What?

THE GIRL. Diaphragms. They got different sizes. You have to get fitted.

CLINTON. What are you talking about?

THE GIRL. Just any one won't do. Did you know that?

42

CLINTON. Get out of here.

THE GIRL. Did you know? I didn't know that Clinton. I got nobody to tell me something like that.

CLINTON. GET THE FUCK OUT OF HERE!

RAY. This was in the summer of infinite heat

The season of unnatural light

When all exposed flesh was seared

And the recycled sun made us cruel

(Lights up on Ernie-Bobo behind the wheel of the car. Clinton works under the hood.)

ERNIE-BOBO. It's hot. Chinese people don't like me.

CLINTON. Try it. *(Ernie-Bobo tries the ignition. Nothing.)*

ERNIE-BOBO. Because Mr. Wong. He doesn't like me.

CLINTON. Listen. You step on the gas.

ERNIE-BOBO. Long one.

CLINTON. You step on the long one. A little. Don't step too hard. It's a bug. Just a little. You squash it. Okay?

ERNIE-BOBO. Yuh-huh.

CLINTON. Okay. *(Ernie-Bobo tries it. Nothing.)* Step on the gas. Step Ernie. You're not stepping.

ERNIE-BOBO. I don't want it to die.

CLINTON. Don't get retarded, okay? Don't be a retard.

ERNIE-BOBO. The luck fell out of me.

CLINTON. Jesus Christ. Slide over. *(Clinton gets behind the wheel. Tries it. Nothing.)* Fuck!

ERNIE-BOBO. 'Cause he doesn't like me. 'Cause he's Chinese.

CLINTON. Look. You gotta do it. I'm gonna turn it. It's gonna go. When I say, you step on the gas.

ERNIE-BOBO. Squash.

CLINTON. Right. Not too hard. Don't do it hard or it'll flood.

ERNIE-BOBO. Okay Clinton. *(Clinton gets back under the hood.)*

CLINTON. Ready?

ERNIE-BOBO. 'Cause he's in the store. Mr. Wong says things on me. He says all the luck fell out of me. 'Cause that's how I am.

CLINTON. Pay attention.

ERNIE-BOBO. Okay. It's hot.

CLINTON. Ernie … Ernie!

ERNIE-BOBO. Yuh-huh.

CLINTON. Pay attention.

ERNIE-BOBO. Okay.

CLINTON. Ready?

43

ERNIE-BOBO. Yeah.

CLINTON. Okay. Hit it. *(Ernie-Bobo tries it. The engine turns over. Once.)* Not too much! Stop! Not to much!

ERNIE-BOBO. Sorry.

CLINTON. Okay. It's okay. Move. *(Clinton climbs in. Short pause.)* Jesus it's hot. Are you hot?

ERNIE-BOBO. Yeah.

CLINTON. Don't drip on the leather.

ERNIE-BOBO. I got sweat in the folds of me Clinton.

CLINTON. It's hot.

ERNIE-BOBO. Yeah.

CLINTON. Be even hotter in Mexico.

ERNIE-BOBO. Yeah.

CLINTON. We can take our shirts off.

ERNIE-BOBO. Yeah.

CLINTON. Go on. It's all right. You can wipe with it. *(Ernie-Bobo takes his shirt off.)*

ERNIE-BOBO. Are we going swimming?

CLINTON. Yeah. We're going swimming.

ERNIE-BOBO. I never swimmed in the dark.

CLINTON. We'll cross the border. We'll disappear. We'll go down by Rosarita. Ernie, the moon keeps the water warm.

ERNIE-BOBO. That's good.

CLINTON. You wanna go?

ERNIE-BOBO. Yeah.

CLINTON. I'm serious. I'll take you.

ERNIE-BOBO. All clear!

CLINTON. No.

ERNIE-BOBO. Faster!

CLINTON. This isn't —

ERNIE-BOBO. Faster Clinton!

CLINTON. No.

ERNIE-BOBO. All clear!

CLINTON. Shut up! Shut the fuck up. This isn't pretend.

ERNIE-BOBO. Oh.

CLINTON. Not tonight.

ERNIE-BOBO. Sorry Clinton.

CLINTON. We're gonna do it amigo. We're gonna get clear. I swear to God.

ERNIE-BOBO. Amigo. Amigo.

CLINTON. Listen.

ERNIE-BOBO. Amigo. Burrito.

CLINTON. Ernie!

ERNIE-BOBO. Yuh-huh.

CLINTON. It's not pretend. Do you understand?

ERNIE-BOBO. Yuh-huh.

CLINTON. We're gonna go. Really go.

ERNIE-BOBO. Bo. Bo. Bo. Bo.

CLINTON. Listen. Are you listening?

ERNIE-BOBO. Bo. Bo. Bo — *(Clinton starts the car. It roars.)* OH MY GOSH! OH MY GOSH CLINTON!

CLINTON. MOTHERFUCKER! DO YOU FEEL THAT! DO YOU FEEL THAT!

ERNIE-BOBO. IT'S IN MY INSIDES!

CLINTON. THAT'S A V-8! DO YOU FEEL THAT! We're gonna get clear. I swear to God. You and me.

ERNIE-BOBO. All clear.

CLINTON. We'll get a brick and throw it through that Chink's window Ernie. I'll do that for you.

ERNIE-BOBO. Okay.

CLINTON. Then we're gone. They'll never find us. Mexico.

ERNIE-BOBO. Okay.

CLINTON. LET'S DO IT! I WANT TO DO IT! DO YOU WANT TO DO IT!

ERNIE-BOBO. DO IT! V-8!

CLINTON. WE'RE GONNA DISAPPEAR! *(Clinton shifts into gear. The engine shuts down.)* No. No. *(He tries it. Nothing.)*

ERNIE-BOBO. DO IT! ALL CLEAR! *(Clinton tries it again. Nothing.)*

CLINTON. No. Come on. Come on!

ERNIE-BOBO. DO IT! DO IT!

CLINTON. No. No. No. No. Please.

ERNIE-BOBO. DO IT! DO IT!

CLINTON. SHUT UP! FUCK!

ERNIE-BOBO. Sorry Clinton.

CLINTON. FUCK! FUCKING FUCK!

ERNIE-BOBO. FUCK!

CLINTON. SHUT UP! I'M — FUCK! I'm gonna fucking die here!

ERNIE-BOBO. Don't die.

CLINTON. Fuck you, you fucking retard! What did you do?

ERNIE-BOBO. I didn't.

CLINTON. WHAT DID YOU DO TO MY FUCKING CAR!

ERNIE-BOBO. Sorry Clinton.

CLINTON. YOU FUCKED MY FUCKING CAR!

ERNIE-BOBO. I didn't!

CLINTON. SHUT UP! *(Clinton hits Ernie-Bobo.)*

ERNIE-BOBO. OWWWW!

CLINTON. SHUT UP! SHUT THE FUCK UP! *(Smack.)*

ERNIE-BOBO. DOOOOON'T!

CLINTON. FUCKING WORTHLESS RETARD! RETARD-ED PIECE OF SHIT! *(Clinton beats Ernie-Bobo.)*

ERNIE-BOBO. DON'T! DON'T!

CLINTON. Open your mouth!

ERNIE-BOBO. No.

CLINTON. OPEN IT! *(Clinton climbs onto Ernie, crushing him down beneath the dash. Clinton begins to undo his belt.)*

ERNIE-BOBO. CLINTON!

CLINTON. Disappear. Disappear.

ERNIE-BOBO. NOOO!

CLINTON. Open your mouth.

(Lights up on Ray-Ray and Angela.)

RAY-RAY. What? What is it?

ANGELA. I heard screaming.

RAY-RAY. I'm here. I'm right here.

ANGELA. Close the blinds.

RAY-RAY. They are closed.

ANGELA. I got scared.

RAY-RAY. It's all right. Tell me.

ANGELA. Dreams.

RAY-RAY. Tell me what you want.

ANGELA. I want.

RAY-RAY. What? You want the pills?

ANGELA. No.

RAY-RAY. Are you in pain?

ANGELA. Yes.

RAY-RAY. Take the pills. I'll get them.

ANGELA. These dreams Raymond. It's like being in a movie.

RAY-RAY. That's nice Mom.

ANGELA. I dream of oceans. Can you see my eyes?

RAY-RAY. It's dark.

ANGELA. I see you perfectly. I'm becoming part of the night.

RAY-RAY. Don't say that.

ANGELA. Come here.

RAY-RAY. I am here.

ANGELA. Closer.

RAY-RAY. Why?

ANGELA. I want to feel you ... Please. *(He moves closer.)* Put your head here.

RAY-RAY. You're sweating.

ANGELA. Please. *(She touches his back.)* My God. You feel wonderful. So substantial ... My God.

RAY-RAY. Mom —

ANGELA. Don't pull away. Please.

RAY-RAY. I don't understand.

ANGELA. Please. I won't say a thing. Just — please. Closer. Here. Put your head here.

RAY-RAY. You have a fever.

ANGELA. It's okay. Put it here. Let me feel you.

RAY-RAY. Mom —

ANGELA. What are you afraid of? I'm dying. Put your head in my lap. *(He does.)* I love this hair. It's your father's hair. Thick and black. Curls. It's the Italian in you. He was Italian. He was foreign and dark. It turned me on.

RAY-RAY. He was Italian?

ANGELA. No. Just his hair.

RAY-RAY. What was he?

ANGELA. I don't know. It never came up. He had the hair. *(She touches his chest.)*

RAY-RAY. What are you doing?

ANGELA. I dream all the time now Raymond.

RAY-RAY. Don't call me that.

ANGELA. Why?

RAY-RAY. That's his name.

ANGELA. It's both your names. You smell like him. Your hair.

RAY-RAY. Shampoo.

ANGELA. Something underneath. An underneath smell. I used to hold his head. We went to watch the ocean. I love the ocean. We sat on the pier. I held his head. I held it here, against my breasts. He was aroused.

RAY-RAY. Mom —

ANGELA. I could taste the salt from my skin in his mouth.

RAY-RAY. Mom —

ANGELA. When he died. There was something sharp. Like a splinter. A pain in the left one. Above my heart ... here. You were

47

born. I held you against my breasts and you suckled me. The pain went away. Do you remember?

RAY-RAY. Of course not.

ANGELA. Sometimes I think you do. It turned into cancer. That's the sort of splinter it was. The piece of him that got embedded in me. It festers. You keep it from killing me.

RAY-RAY. I don't.

ANGELA. You do. It grows when you're not with me — when you leave.

RAY-RAY. I'm not leaving. I'll never leave you.

ANGELA. Come closer.

RAY-RAY. What are you doing? *(She pulls him to her chest.)*

ANGELA. Right here. Right between them.

RAY-RAY. Stop.

ANGELA. This part of me. Right here. This part is alive.

RAY-RAY. Let go.

ANGELA. Right here. Hold me.

RAY-RAY. No.

ANGELA. Please.

RAY-RAY. LET GO! *(He breaks away.)*

ANGELA. I'm sorry.

RAY-RAY. It's okay.

ANGELA. You don't understand.

RAY-RAY. You're not yourself.

ANGELA. You don't understand.

RAY-RAY. I'll get your pills.

ANGELA. I love you because you're him. I loved him because he was you. You're the same.

RAY-RAY. We're not the same.

ANGELA. You're both my life.

RAY-RAY. Don't talk. I'll be right back. *(Ray-Ray exits.)*

ANGELA. There is no time. *(Ray-Ray enters with pills and water.)*

RAY-RAY. Here. Green and blue.

ANGELA. I don't think so.

RAY-RAY. Yes.

ANGELA. No.

RAY-RAY. Don't be difficult.

ANGELA. It's all right. Do you see?

RAY-RAY. Take this.

ANGELA. You don't see it, do you? It's perfect.

RAY-RAY. Take this. You'll feel better.

48

ANGELA. It's a perfect world. Green and blue and balanced between spiders and birds. The light. Darkness. That's his dominion. I could never paint him. I couldn't make his shape with my hand.

RAY-RAY. Shhh …

ANGELA. The spider.

RAY-RAY. Don't talk. Here.

ANGELA. I feel my life so strongly now. There is love. I felt love. I feel love Raymond.

RAY-RAY. You're crying.

ANGELA. I'm crying.

RAY-RAY. Don't cry.

ANGELA. It's so blue Raymond.

RAY-RAY. Don't cry.

ANGELA. I was sitting on the pier. You touched my breasts. I was a girl. You kissed me. I was a girl. Your kiss was everything.

RAY-RAY. My heart.

ANGELA. Kiss me.

RAY-RAY. My heart hurts.

ANGELA. Kiss me. *(Pause.)* Kiss me Raymond. I want to dream of oceans. *(A pause. He kisses her deeply. Ray-Ray sits on the car. A pause. Clinton enters with a box of assorted possessions.)*

CLINTON. Get off of there. *(Ray-Ray does. Clinton pops the hood.)* I don't like people in here when I'm not around. You know that.

RAY-RAY. I saw your light.

CLINTON. Get the door. *(Ray-Ray opens the car door. Clinton puts the box in the car.)*

RAY-RAY. I saw you moving.

CLINTON. God damn right you did. *(Clinton exits. He reenters with a small box and a can of oil.)*

RAY-RAY. I need you Clinton.

CLINTON. What? Are you stoned?

RAY-RAY. No.

CLINTON. Your eyes are fucked up. *(Clinton loads the box. Exits. He reenters and slides under the car. He slides out with a tray full of spent oil, which he places on the roof of the car. He pours the new oil into the engine and slams the hood.)* You gonna shake my hand?

RAY-RAY. Clinton — *(Clinton begins jacking up the car.)*

CLINTON. I got the bolt for the transmission today. It connects the drive train to the trannie. Which connects to the wheels. Which connects to the road. Which connects to Mexico. Which connects to me.

49

RAY-RAY. Mexico.

CLINTON. That's right Ray. I'm gone. This is yours.

RAY-RAY. What is?

CLINTON. My kingdom man.

RAY-RAY. Oh.

CLINTON I'm the king. You the prince. You're gonna be the king.

RAY-RAY. I need you to come to my house.

CLINTON. What?

RAY-RAY. Come to my house.

CLINTON. Am I talking to myself? I'm going to Mexico Ray. Not tomorrow. Not next week. I'm going now. I don't have time for social visits.

RAY-RAY. She's dead.

CLINTON. What?

RAY-RAY. She messed herself. I tried to clean her but I — Her eyes are stuck open.

CLINTON. Ray —

RAY-RAY. I can't get her clothes on Clinton. I tried. She's cold. I couldn't —

CLINTON. Ah fuck.

RAY-RAY. I didn't cry. Just like you said. I didn't but — I can't … I need you to come over and shut her eyes. Sit her up —

CLINTON. Wait —

RAY-RAY. Clean her. Put her clothes on. Sit her up so I can do her face —

CLINTON. Hold on. You need some help here.

RAY-RAY. Yes.

CLINTON. No. Slow down. You need paramedics or something.

RAY-RAY. No.

CLINTON. 911. You call 911?

RAY-RAY. My shoulders hurt, just like you said. My balls —

CLINTON. Ray —

RAY-RAY. I tried to clean her. There was a sound —

CLINTON. Get a —

RAY-RAY. A sound inside me Clinton. Here. A sound like crack —

CLINTON. Ray —

RAY-RAY. Crack — Cracking sound. Here. And I knew if I touched her —

CLINTON. Calm down.

RAY-RAY. I knew — I knew I was gonna break apart. I'm gonna break apart.

CLINTON. You're not gonna break apart. Calm down.

RAY-RAY. I need you to come to my house.

CLINTON. No —

RAY-RAY. Please.

CLINTON. Come on Ray.

RAY-RAY. Oh God Clinton please.

CLINTON. What is it you want me to do? You want me to go over there and what?

RAY-RAY. Put her clothes —

CLINTON. No. No. What are you talking? This is not my thing. I can't deal with dead … forget it. Look Ray, this is not my thing. This is your thing —

RAY-RAY. No —

CLINTON. Mexico is my thing. Your thing Ray. Your mom —

RAY-RAY. I can't — Oh God.

CLINTON. You can —

RAY-RAY. Oh God.

CLINTON. Yes you can. Look at me. You can. I know you can. Look at me. Ray. Look at me.

RAY-RAY. I got nobody.

CLINTON. This … This takes a man Ray. That's what's needed here.

RAY-RAY. I got you.

CLINTON. Stop it! You are a man Ray. And a man does what needs to be done. You're a man right? Am I right? *(Beat.)* You are Ray. I know you are. You know how I know? Ray? Because I made you one. Now you go over there, you put her clothes on. You take your hands —

RAY-RAY. No —

CLINTON. You take your hands and shut her eyes —

RAY-RAY. I can't … *(Ray-Ray starts to cry. Clinton seizes him by the arms and begins to shake him violently.)*

CLINTON. WHAT ARE YOU DOING? WHAT ARE YOU FUCKING DOING? YOU DO NOT PUSS OUT ON ME! DO NOT FUCKING CAVE! DON'T! You go over there! You fucking clean her! You make her up nice! YOU CLOSE HER FUCKING EYES! Then you — then — call the cops! Or, or, or, I DON'T KNOW WHO YOU FUCKING CALL BUT YOU QUIT YOUR FUCKING BLUBBERING AND CALL THEM! *(Clinton releases Ray-Ray who stumbles back a little, sucking air.)*

RAY-RAY. Help me.

CLINTON. I'm going to Mexico Ray. I'm gone. I'm not even here right now. And we are not talking. And I don't have any ideas about dead people because I don't even know you anymore.

RAY-RAY. What are you?

CLINTON. What?

RAY-RAY. What are you?

CLINTON. Go home.

RAY-RAY. When you were on me — I was under you — You marked me. In my mouth. I was numb —

CLINTON. What?

RAY-RAY. Your spit. My mouth. My hands. I couldn't feel my hands —

CLINTON. Hey —

RAY-RAY. I felt a hot thing in me. My guts all hot and trying to come up my throat. Like a volcano —

CLINTON. Calm down.

RAY-RAY. Was it poison?

CLINTON. What?

RAY-RAY. Venom.

CLINTON. You're caving in Ray.

RAY-RAY. You break everything Clinton.

CLINTON. Get out of here.

RAY-RAY. I watch you. You break everything.

CLINTON. I'm gonna break you if you don't get the fuck out of here. *(Clinton takes the bolt from the box. He gets the mechanic's trolley. He looks at Ray-Ray. Clinton slides under the car.)* Go home. *(A pause. Ray-Ray looks at the oil pan. He dips his finger into it and begins to smear the used black oil on his face. He gets up and walks to the jack that supports the car.)* Go home Ray-Ray. Go take care of your mom. *(Pause.)* Don't piss me off man. I can see your fucking feet. You got three seconds. I'm gonna count to three. Ray? *(Short pause.)* One … Two … *(Ray-Ray releases the jack. A massive metal sound. Lights shift red. Clinton's leg kicks. He begins to scream. It fades into pained sounds. Then nothing.)*

RAY-RAY. Shhh … It's all right. Everything's broken now Clinton. I see it in the sidewalk. That's where it shows. 'Cause of the heat. The way it makes everything push against everything. It cracks. The concrete. Where we put our hands. It's all broken. *(Clinton's leg kicks again.)* Shhh. Don't. Don't. It's all right. I know how it is. Something push down on you so hard that you can't even breathe. Can't get air to cry out. To cry. Don't cry. Let's just be quiet now. I

52

feel the part of you that trickled down my throat. I feel it here. This is where it grows. It hurts. I got you inside me. Like you said. And you got me. And we know what each other is and who eats who, right? And we don't fucking cry. *(Clinton's foot moves. Ray-Ray kneels and looks under the car.)* It's all right now. You just be quiet. It's your head see. It's got the wrong shape. Your fucking eye came out Clinton. Came right out of your head. And your ribs popped loose. And there's bubbles. You remember when you skinned your knee on the drive? Just a little boy crying over your knee and it was skinned so bad there wasn't even blood, just that new white-white skin underneath. Your mom took you inside. And there was your skin on the driveway right next to me. You remember that? I touched it. It was all spongy and warm like it was still a part of you and alive. And I touched it and I wanted to know what you looked like inside. 'Cause inside, I knew you were the same color as me. We're the same. I crushed a widow once. It left blood and black shit all over the back of my trowel. So that's how I knew what color we were. You're black inside Clinton. I'm black inside. I can see it now. I guess. It looks black. I don't know. Maybe that's just the oil. I can't tell. It's dark underneath. And I can't tell if it's blood or if it's oil Clinton. I can't tell the oil from the blood.

(Lights up on Ernie-Bobo and The Girl.)

ERNIE-BOBO. You waiting for the six-five? I'm waiting for the six-five. It's not here.

THE GIRL. No shit.

ERNIE-BOBO. It's not here. Sometimes I come and it's here. It waits for me sometimes. Sometimes I don't have a dollar. *(Short pause.)* When I don't have a dollar, I walk. It takes longer to walk. And there's cars. *(Short pause.)* Clinton has a car. You ride in Clinton's car?

THE GIRL. He's gone.

ERNIE-BOBO. But sometimes. 'Cause sometimes I see you in Clinton's car. In the back. He drives you.

THE GIRL. That's was his Mom's.

ERNIE-BOBO. Okay The Girl. But remember? Remember when I was walking?

THE GIRL. I don't want to talk now Ernie.

ERNIE-BOBO. Okay. But remember? You and Clinton and Ray-Ray? You got out of the car — Remember? And Ray-Ray said things on me. And Clinton pulled my pants down. And it was funny. Pants down is funny sometimes. Remember?

THE GIRL. Man —

ERNIE-BOBO. And you and Ray-Ray was laughing. And Clinton was laughing. 'Cause pants down is funny. And Clinton said he was going to shave my boy parts. And I was walking home.

THE GIRL. You shouldn't laugh at that. It's not funny.

ERNIE-BOBO. You laughed.

THE GIRL. It wasn't that kind of laugh.

ERNIE-BOBO. What kind of laugh was it?

THE GIRL. Shut up, okay?

ERNIE-BOBO. I only know one kind of laugh … Where are you going?

THE GIRL. Hospital.

ERNIE-BOBO. Are you sick?

THE GIRL. Something like that.

ERNIE-BOBO. You call 911?

THE GIRL. No.

ERNIE-BOBO. It's for emergencies.

THE GIRL. Thanks.

ERNIE-BOBO. Clinton's gone?

THE GIRL. I guess.

ERNIE-BOBO. He go to Mexico?

THE GIRL. I guess. I don't know.

ERNIE-BOBO. The moon keeps the water warm.

THE GIRL. I hate Mexico.

ERNIE-BOBO. In Mexico, you swim at night, in Mexico.

THE GIRL. Shut up Ernie.

ERNIE-BOBO. Okay.

THE GIRL. I don't want to hear any fucking Mexico talk.

ERNIE-BOBO. I say the wrong things.

THE GIRL. That's because you're retarded. No offense, but your mom screwed her brother or some shit like that.

ERNIE-BOBO. Okay The Girl.

THE GIRL. And don't call me that, okay? I don't get called that anymore. My name is Jenette.

ERNIE-BOBO. Jenette.

THE GIRL. Right.

ERNIE-BOBO. It's pretty.

THE GIRL. Why do they call you that?

ERNIE-BOBO. What?

THE GIRL. Why do they call you Bobo?

ERNIE-BOBO. 'Cause of the before school. Which is where the

sandbox is. 'Cause I didn't know words. I didn't know words then, so I did my bobo. *(Sing-song.)* Bo, bo, bo, bo, bo, bo, bo ... 'Cause Bobo is funny sometimes. And it's a word now. Bobo is a word.

THE GIRL. It got on your skin.

ERNIE-BOBO. Yes. It got on my skin. I don't remember. But sometimes things get on my skin. I can never get them off. I'm Ernie-Bobo now. 'Cause bobo is funny sometimes. *(It begins to snow. the Girl catches the flakes in her hand and looks up.)*

THE GIRL. What the hell?

ERNIE-BOBO. OH MY GOSH! OH MY GOSH IT'S SNOW-ING!

THE GIRL. Beautiful.

ERNIE-BOBO. OH MY GOSH! SNOWING! OH MY GOSH! OH MY GOSH! *(Ernie-Bobo lays on the ground and begins to make snow angels. the Girl laughs. Ernie-Bobo is delighted.)*

THE GIRL. What are you doing? *(Lights shift and begin a slow fade.)*
On the day of his leaving
A thousand miles north
St. Helen burst her rocky seams
She cast her embers to the atmosphere
They drifted
And fell down on us like snow
This was in the summer of infinite heat
On the morning of my bloom
In the land of spiders and birds
I seldom think of them
Sometimes they come to me in dreams
But I remember that morning
And the way I held my head
And I remember the gentle boy
Making angels in the ash. *(Fade to black.)*

End of Play

PROPERTY LIST

Road map
Glass of water
Tray of food
Fork
Toolbox
Mechanics trolley
Wrench
Screwdriver
Greasy towel
Oil pan
Car jack
Tray of paints and brushes
Nail polish
Cigarettes
Pills
Box of assorted possessions
Smaller box
Can of oil

NEW PLAYS

★ **THE EXONERATED by Jessica Blank and Erik Jensen.** Six interwoven stories paint a picture of an American criminal justice system gone horribly wrong and six brave souls who persevered to survive it. "The #1 play of the year...intense and deeply affecting..." *–NY Times.* "Riveting. Simple, honest storytelling that demands reflection." *–A.P.* "Artful and moving...pays tribute to the resilience of human hearts and minds." *–Variety.* "Stark...riveting...cunningly orchestrated." *–The New Yorker.* "Hard-hitting, powerful, and socially relevant." *–Hollywood Reporter.* [7M, 3W] ISBN: 0-8222-1946-8

★ **STRING FEVER by Jacquelyn Reingold.** Lily juggles the big issues: turning forty, artificial insemination and the elusive scientific Theory of Everything in this Off-Broadway comedy hit. "Applies the elusive rules of string theory to the conundrums of one woman's love life. Think *Sex and the City* meets *Copenhagen.*" *–NY Times.* "A funny offbeat and touching look at relationships...an appealing romantic comedy populated by oddball characters." *–NY Daily News.* "Where kooky, zany, and madcap meet...whimsically winsome." *–NY Magazine.* "STRING FEVER will have audience members happily stringing along." *–TheaterMania.com.* "Reingold's language is surprising, inventive, and unique." *–nytheatre.com.* "...[a] whimsical comic voice." *–Time Out.* [3M, 3W (doubling)] ISBN: 0-8222-1952-2

★ **DEBBIE DOES DALLAS adapted by Erica Schmidt, composed by Andrew Sherman, conceived by Susan L. Schwartz.** A modern morality tale told as a comic musical of tragic proportions as the classic film is brought to the stage. "A scream! A saucy, tongue-in-cheek romp." *–The New Yorker.* "Hilarious! DEBBIE manages to have it all: beauty, brains and a great sense of humor!" *–Time Out.* "Shamelessly silly, shrewdly self-aware and proud of being naughty. Great fun!" *–NY Times.* "Racy and raucous, a lighthearted, fast-paced thoroughly engaging and hilarious send-up." *–NY Daily News.* [3M, 5W] ISBN: 0-8222-1955-7

★ **THE MYSTERY PLAYS by Roberto Aguirre-Sacasa.** Two interrelated one acts, loosely based on the tradition of the medieval mystery plays. "... stylish, spine-tingling...Mr. Aguirre-Sacasa uses standard tricks of horror stories, borrowing liberally from masters like Kafka, Lovecraft, Hitchock...But his mastery of the genre is his own...irresistible." *–NY Times.* "Undaunted by the special-effects limitations of theatre, playwright and *Marvel* comic-book writer Roberto Aguirre-Sacasa maps out some creepy twilight zones in THE MYSTERY PLAYS, an engaging, related pair of one acts...The theatre may rarely deliver shocks equivalent to, say, *Dawn of the Dead*, but Aguirre-Sacasa's work is fine compensation." *–Time Out.* [4M, 2W] ISBN: 0-8222-2038-5

★ **THE JOURNALS OF MIHAIL SEBASTIAN by David Auburn.** This epic one-man play spans eight tumultuous years and opens a uniquely personal window on the Romanian Holocaust and the Second World War. "Powerful." *–NY Times.* "[THE JOURNALS OF MIHAIL SEBASTIAN] allows us to glimpse the idiosyncratic effects of that awful history on one intelligent, pragmatic, recognizably real man..." *–NY Newsday.* [3M, 5W] ISBN: 0-8222-2006-7

★ **LIVING OUT by Lisa Loomer.** The story of the complicated relationship between a Salvadoran nanny and the Anglo lawyer she works for. "A stellar new play. Searingly funny." *–The New Yorker.* "Both generous and merciless, equally enjoyable and disturbing." *–NY Newsday.* "A bitingly funny new comedy. The plight of working mothers is explored from two pointedly contrasting perspectives in this sympathetic, sensitive new play." *–Variety.* [2M, 6W] ISBN: 0-8222-1994-8

DRAMATISTS PLAY SERVICE, INC.
440 Park Avenue South, New York, NY 10016 212-683-8960 Fax 212-213-1539
postmaster@dramatists.com www.dramatists.com

NEW PLAYS

★ **MATCH by Stephen Belber.** Mike and Lisa Davis interview a dancer and choreographer about his life, but it is soon evident that their agenda will either ruin or inspire them—and definitely change their lives forever. "Prolific laughs and ear-to-ear smiles." *–NY Magazine.* "Uproariously funny, deeply moving, enthralling theater. Stephen Belber's MATCH has great beauty and tenderness, and abounds in wit." *–NY Daily News.* "Three and a half out of four stars." *–USA Today.* "A theatrical steeplechase that leads straight from outrageous bitchery to unadorned, heartfelt emotion." *–Wall Street Journal.* [2M, 1W] ISBN: 0-8222-2020-1

★ **HANK WILLIAMS: LOST HIGHWAY by Randal Myler and Mark Harelik.** The story of the beloved and volatile country-music legend Hank Williams, featuring twenty-five of his most unforgettable songs. "[LOST HIGHWAY has] the exhilarating feeling of Williams on stage in a particular place on a particular night…serves up classic country with the edges raw and the energy hot…By the end of the play, you've traveled on a profound emotional journey: LOST HIGHWAY transports its audience and communicates the inspiring message of the beauty and richness of Williams' songs…forceful, clear-eyed, moving, impressive." *–Rolling Stone.* "…honors a very particular musical talent with care and energy… smart, sweet, poignant." *–NY Times.* [7M, 3W] ISBN: 0-8222-1985-9

★ **THE STORY by Tracey Scott Wilson.** An ambitious black newspaper reporter goes against her editor to investigate a murder and finds the *best* story…but at what cost? "A singular new voice…deeply emotional, deeply intellectual, and deeply musical…" *–The New Yorker.* "…a conscientious and absorbing new drama…" *–NY Times.* "…a riveting, tough-minded drama about race, reporting and the truth…" *–A.P.* "… a stylish, attention-holding script that ends on a chilling note that will leave viewers with much to talk about." *–Curtain Up.* [2M, 7W (doubling, flexible casting)] ISBN: 0-8222-1998-0

★ **OUR LADY OF 121st STREET by Stephen Adly Guirgis.** The body of Sister Rose, beloved Harlem nun, has been stolen, reuniting a group of life-challenged childhood friends who square off as they wait for her return. "A scorching and dark new comedy… Mr. Guirgis has one of the finest imaginations for dialogue to come along in years." *–NY Times.* "Stephen Guirgis may be the best playwright in America under forty." *–NY Magazine.* [8M, 4W] ISBN: 0-8222-1965-4

★ **HOLLYWOOD ARMS by Carrie Hamilton and Carol Burnett.** The coming-of-age story of a dreamer who manages to escape her bleak life and follow her romantic ambitions to stardom. Based on Carol Burnett's bestselling autobiography, *One More Time.* "…pure theatre and pure entertainment…" *–Talkin' Broadway.* "…a warm, fuzzy evening of theatre." *–BrodwayBeat.com.* "…chuckles and smiles of recognition or surprise flow naturally…a remarkable slice of life." *–TheatreScene.net.* [5M, 5W, 1 girl] ISBN: 0-8222-1959-X

★ **INVENTING VAN GOGH by Steven Dietz.** A haunting and hallucinatory drama about the making of art, the obsession to create and the fine line that separates truth from myth. "Like a van Gogh painting, Dietz's story is a gorgeous example of excess—one that remakes reality with broad, well-chosen brush strokes. At evening's end, we're left with the author's resounding opinions on art and artifice, and provoked by his constant query into which is greater: van Gogh's art or his violent myth." *–Phoenix New Times.* "Dietz's writing is never simple. It is always brilliant. Shaded, compressed, direct, lucid—he frames his subject with a remarkable understanding of painting as a physical experience." *–Tucson Citizen.* [4M, 1W] ISBN: 0-8222-1954-9

DRAMATISTS PLAY SERVICE, INC.
440 Park Avenue South, New York, NY 10016 212-683-8960 Fax 212-213-1539
postmaster@dramatists.com www.dramatists.com

NEW PLAYS

★ **INTIMATE APPAREL by Lynn Nottage.** The moving and lyrical story of a turn-of-the-century black seamstress whose gifted hands and sewing machine are the tools she uses to fashion her dreams from the whole cloth of her life's experiences. "…Nottage's play has a delicacy and eloquence that seem absolutely right for the time she is depicting…" –*NY Daily News*. "…thoughtful, affecting…The play offers poignant commentary on an era when the cut and color of one's dress—and of course, skin—determined whom one could and could not marry, sleep with, even talk to in public." –*Variety*. [2M, 4W] ISBN: 0-8222-2009-1

★ **BROOKLYN BOY by Donald Margulies.** A witty and insightful look at what happens to a writer when his novel hits the bestseller list. "The characters are beautifully drawn, the dialogue sparkles…" –*nytheatre.com*. "Few playwrights have the mastery to smartly investigate so much through a laugh-out-loud comedy that combines the vintage subject matter of successful writer-returning-to-ethnic-roots with the familiar mid-life crisis." –*Show Business Weekly*. [4M, 3W] ISBN: 0-8222-2074-1

★ **CROWNS by Regina Taylor.** Hats become a springboard for an exploration of black history and identity in this celebratory musical play. "Taylor pulls off a Hat Trick: She scores thrice, turning CROWNS into an artful amalgamation of oral history, fashion show, and musical theater…" –*TheatreMania.com*. "…wholly theatrical…Ms. Taylor has created a show that seems to arise out of spontaneous combustion, as if a bevy of department-store customers simultaneously decided to stage a revival meeting in the changing room." –*NY Times*. [1M, 6W (2 musicians)] ISBN: 0-8222-1963-8

★ **EXITS AND ENTRANCES by Athol Fugard.** The story of a relationship between a young playwright on the threshold of his career and an aging actor who has reached the end of his. "[Fugard] can say more with a single line than most playwrights convey in an entire script…Paraphrasing the title, it's safe to say this drama, making its memorable entrance into our consciousness, is unlikely to exit as long as a theater exists for exceptional work." –*Variety*. "A thought-provoking, elegant and engrossing new play…" –*Hollywood Reporter*. [2M] ISBN: 0-8222-2041-5

★ **BUG by Tracy Letts.** A thriller featuring a pair of star-crossed lovers in an Oklahoma City motel facing a bug invasion, paranoia, conspiracy theories and twisted psychological motives. "…obscenely exciting…top-flight craftsmanship. Buckle up and brace yourself…" –*NY Times*. "…[a] thoroughly outrageous and thoroughly entertaining play…the possibility of enemies, real and imagined, to squash has never been more theatrical." –*A.P.* [3M, 2W] ISBN: 0-8222-2016-4

★ **THOM PAIN (BASED ON NOTHING) by Will Eno.** An ordinary man muses on childhood, yearning, disappointment and loss, as he draws the audience into his last-ditch plea for empathy and enlightenment. "It's one of those treasured nights in the theater—treasured nights anywhere, for that matter—that can leave you both breathless with exhilaration and…in a puddle of tears." –*NY Times*. "Eno's words…are familiar, but proffered in a way that is constantly contradictory to our expectations. Beckett is certainly among his literary ancestors." –*nytheatre.com*. [1M] ISBN: 0-8222-2076-8

★ **THE LONG CHRISTMAS RIDE HOME by Paula Vogel.** Past, present and future collide on a snowy Christmas Eve for a troubled family of five. "…[a] lovely and hauntingly original family drama…a work that breathes so much life into the theater." –*Time Out*. "…[a] delicate visual feast…" –*NY Times*. "…brutal and lovely…the overall effect is magical." –*NY Newsday*. [3M, 3W] ISBN: 0-8222-2003-2

DRAMATISTS PLAY SERVICE, INC.
440 Park Avenue South, New York, NY 10016 212-683-8960 Fax 212-213-1539
postmaster@dramatists.com   www.dramatists.com